THE LIFE STORY OF A BARN

by Frank Coffin
illustrated by William Ersland

Harcourt
SCHOOL PUBLISHERS

Requests for permission to make copies of any part of the work should be addressed to School Permissions and Copyrights, Harcourt, Inc., 6277 Sea Harbor Drive, Orlando, Florida 32887-6777. Fax: 407-345-2418.

HARCOURT and the Harcourt Logo are trademarks of Harcourt, Inc., registered in the United States of America and/or other jurisdictions.

Printed in Mexico

ISBN 10: 0-15-350677-6
ISBN 13: 978-0-15-350677-2

Ordering Options
ISBN 10: 0-15-350600-8 (Grade 3 On-Level Collection)
ISBN 13: 978-0-15-350600-0 (Grade 3 On-Level Collection)
ISBN 10: 0-15-357898-X (package of 5)
ISBN 13: 978-0-15-357898-4 (package of 5)

9 10 0908 12 11 10 09

The man needed a new barn. His little farm was growing. He had cleared new land and built new fences. He wanted a better place to keep animals and to store tools.

There were no companies to build barns in the 1880s. The man and his sons planned the barn together. They made drawings and lists of things they would need. They wanted to build the barn into the side of a hill.

The man and his sons carried stones from the fields. They built low walls for the base. The two sides were the same, leading up into the slope of the hill. Spaces were left for windows. The third side had a gap in it for a door. The walls had to be exactly even so that the barn would stand straight. It took a long time and a lot of work for the three of them to get the walls just right.

Neighbors and friends came to help next. They brought food so that everyone could stay all day. The men helped to set heavy beams on top of the walls. Then they all worked together to raise the frame of the barn. It was a day of hard work.

In some places, people stayed until the whole barn was done. Here, though, the neighbors just helped build the frame. Over the next few weeks, the farmer and his sons nailed up siding and then row upon row of wooden shingles for the roof.

It was not a big barn. The man had only a few animals to keep. The lower part would be cooler in summer. It would stay warmer in winter, too. Some animals would stay there.

The farmer's tools and equipment were on the main level. He could drive his wagon right up the slope and through the big door. He kept his horses in stalls there, too.

The top level was for hay. A lot of work went into growing, cutting, and storing enough hay to get the animals through the winter. The big hay wagon made many trips to the barn through the three cuttings of hay every summer.

The years went by, and the barn did its job. It was a home to many animals.

One of the man's sons stayed on the farm. He, too, lived his life near the barn. When he was an old man, he told children stories about building the barn. Then one of his sons kept the little farm as the years passed.

Life continued in the barn. Many families of ducks and geese waddled nearby. Cows mooed each morning and evening. Chickens pecked around the yard, and a proud rooster greeted everyone each morning.

The barn stood through cold winters and hot summers. Slowly, the barn changed. It needed some work. After countless rainstorms, the old wooden roof began to leak. The barn got a new metal roof of shiny tin. The boards got new coats of red barn paint. Sagging doors got new braces. A new machine called a tractor replaced the wagon. The farmer would not give up his horses, though. He did not suppose that farming would change that much.

Thirty more years went by on the farm. A bigger tractor was purchased. A shed went up to cover a hay baler. There were still horses, but they were no longer workhorses.

Year after year after year, animals were born in the barn. Kittens played in the hay. The mice they chased hid in the floors. Swallows nested under the eaves. Pigs rested in the cool earth below. Cattle went out and came in, morning and night. Life continued in the barn.

More years went by, and finally, the farm
slowed down. There were fewer animals. A big
tractor mostly sat. A small farm like this could
no longer earn enough money to feed a family. At
last, the farm failed. The farm machines were sold.
The great-great grandson of the barn's builder
moved to the city for a new job. The barn fell
silent after almost one hundred years.

Time strikes hard at a barn that no one fixes. Rust on a nail hole loosened part of the roof. Then the wind blew a piece of the roof away. Rain and snow blew in. Water and frost cracked the stone base. In a few winters, more water froze and broke the base. The frame of the old barn began to sag. Paint peeled, and boards dried and shrank in the summer sun. Nails began to pull. More weather worked its way inside the old barn.

The land lay empty for more seasons. The fields grew over with briars and brush. Groundhogs moved into the lower level of the barn. Birds roosted on the bare rafters. The barn leaned further. Its own weight began to damage it even more. The rest of the roof blew away, and the timbers rotted.

The barn became a skeleton. What was once a haven for farm life was now just a glimpse of the past. One sunny afternoon, without warning, the barn fell. It went down gently, quietly, as if it were settling to rest.

Nothing looks like a barn there anymore. Summers still come, and wild flowers grow. Swallows still catch insects in midair. A weed spears a rotting board. Rabbits run a maze among the old boards, and a fox comes sniffing through them once in a while. Snakes hatch among the falling stones. They watch for field mice that burrow into the soft earth under what was once something else. Life continues, but never exactly in the same way.

Think Critically

1. What details does the author give about the neighbors and friends who helped to build the barn?

2. Name some ways that the pictures in the book shows time passing on the farm.

3. What does the author mean when he says, "Time strikes hard at a barn that no one fixes"?

4. From what you read, about how many years do you think the barn stood?

5. How do you think the author feels about the old barn?

Science

Making Hay Hay was used to feed the animals in the story. Find out some more about hay. What is it? How is it grown and harvested? Make a diagram showing the steps that it takes to get hay to feed animals.

 School-Home Connection Old buildings remind us of the people who came before us. Ask family and friends to tell about old buildings they know or that they remember. What do the buildings tell about the people who used them?

Word Count: 944